Play
Therapy

Play Therapy

written by
Michael Joseph

illustrated by
R.W. Alley

Abbey Press

Published by One Caring Place
Abbey Press
St. Meinrad, Indiana 47577

Library of Congress Catalog Number
90-85709

ISBN 0-87029-233-1

Printed in the United States of America

Foreword

We live in a serious world. For too many of us, work is competitively cut-throat, social expectations are high, parenting is a burden, and marriage is a project. Religion is solemn and our "recreation" is largely of the spectator variety. If this isn't enough, we project our success-driven and labor-based ethic onto children, pressuring them—albeit inadvertently—to learn, achieve, and succeed almost from infancy. Is it any wonder that we become bored, tired, and frustrated by life and our children become candidates for depression at an early age?

Why do we live this way? Is it perhaps because we've forgotten the importance of play? We stake too much of our personal value and dignity on what we do and accomplish. We overorganize and overanalyze our lives. In the process we forget that life is a gift as well as a task. If we are to enjoy this gift and truly *live* our lives, we'd best learn to play authentically once again.

Play Therapy is designed as your first playmate on the way to reawakening your inner child. Use the thirty-five delightful rules and illustrations in these pages as reminders and encouragement to rediscover your playful self. You will find that play, indeed, is the therapy for every stress and challenge; even better, it is the best preventive medicine.

1.

Childhood is life's first gift.
Whatever your age,
acknowledge your child within.

2.

Play is the birthright of your child within. Do it often to know discovery, wonderment, and delight.

3.

Let your child within run free.
A child kept from play is an
abused child.

4.

It's OK to play and be happy.
In the beginning, God played
with infinite possibilities—
including you—and it
was good.

5.

Remember: you have intrinsic value and goodness. You don't have to prove it by ceaseless productivity.

6.

Consider playfulness as a gift
from heaven. After all, only
people with faith can play.
Others must work and worry.

7.

Play is natural exhilaration.
Don't confuse it with shopping,
eating, or artificial excitements.

8.

Give quality time and fresh energy to play. Play shouldn't be an afterthought.

9.

Be spontaneous. Though
risky, it opens up a world of
exciting possibilities.

10.

Get out of doors every day.
A field of dreams awaits you.

11.

Let the wind blow in your face; breathe deeply. The wind's caress will re-create you.

12.

Let your hair down. Rigid folk are intruders on the field of play.

13.

Let your hands get dirty; let your hair get mussed. In play, carelessness is a virtue.

14.

Notice the playfulness of nature:
gurgling streams, dancing light,
humming birds, fluttering
leaves, twinkling stars.
All creation wants to play
with you.

15.

Respond to your pet's playful appeals. They are reminders that now is the only moment you have.

16.

Clown around. A little levity can bring a smile to the overserious.

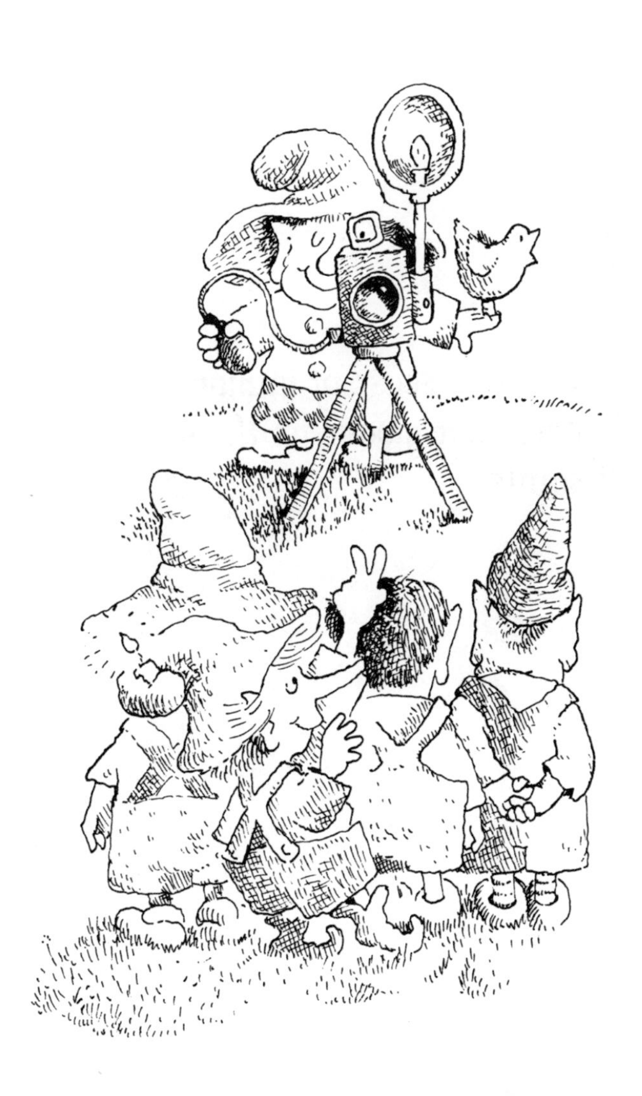

17.

Cultivate a sense of humor.
Humor, not gloom, is the secret
of saints.

18.

Be flexible. Letting go of plans and schedules will bring a treasure of new experiences to your door.

19.

Adopt a hobby, take up a sport, pursue your dream—just for the fun of it. Play makes no demand to succeed or win, only to enjoy.

20.

Accept limitations. Art and invention come from people who play with limited resources.

21.

Work playfully. Play isn't what you do, but how creatively and freely you do it.

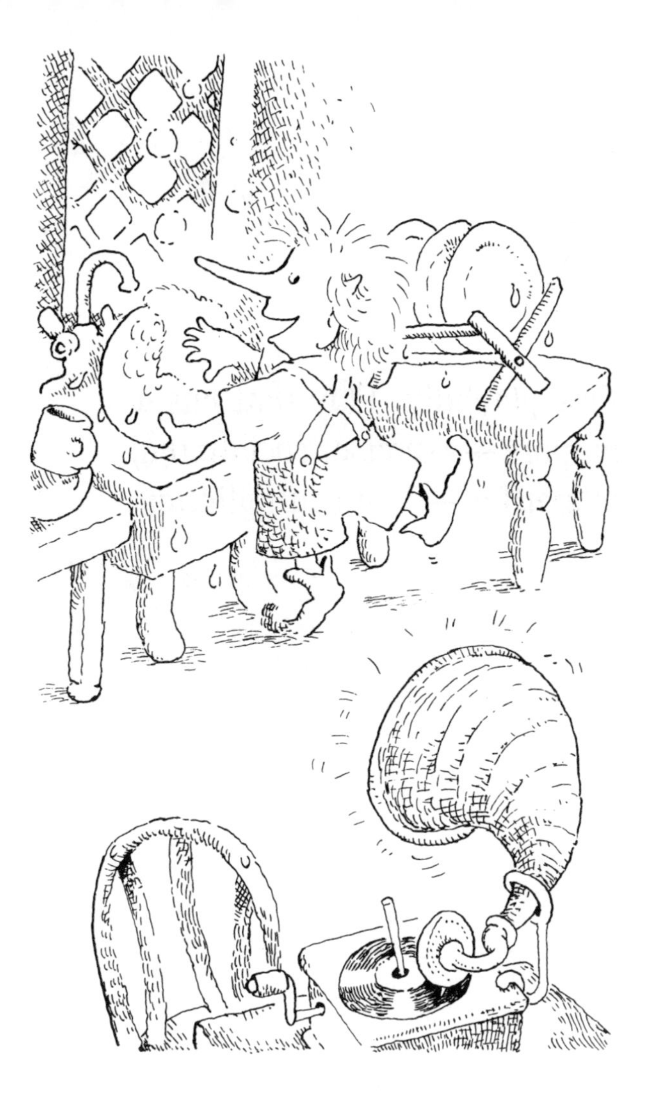

22.

Play playfully. Play that has a purpose—exercise, socializing, relaxation—is a contradiction.

23.

Befriend people who bring out the playful side of you. They are a gift beyond measure.

24.

Give free play to your imagination. Creativity is what makes you human.

25.

Play alone. Solitude fosters wonderment.

26.

Play with others. The push and pull of playing together will enlarge your vision and sharpen your talents.

27.

Remember the most playful— and happy—activities of your childhood. Try them again!

28.

Dance, skip, get physical! You were designed to live in the body, not just the head.

29.

Play with obstacles, don't go around them. The challenge will draw out your full potential.

30.

*Play with color, form, light,
shadows, space, sound, words,
silence, taste, smells.
Everywhere is a playground.*

31.

Play the fool. Fools serve the world by unveiling its pretense and fakery.

FUN

32.

Let go of preconceived notions and prejudices. Expect surprises; expect miracles.

33.

Laugh at yourself. A healthy acceptance of your idiosyncrasies, mistakes, and mishaps can be a gift to others.

34.

Think of play as a preview of Paradise: time disappears, self-consciousness shrinks, and fulfillment prevails.

35.

Creating a richer, fuller life is child's play. It's never too late to have a happy childhood.

Michael Joseph is the pen name of a writer who works and plays in the hills of southern Indiana. His background includes graduate research on the role of humor and play in religion.

Illustrator for the Abbey Press Elf-help Books, **R.W. Alley** also illustrates and writes children's books. He lives in Barrington, Rhode Island, with his wife, daughter, and son.

The Story of the Abbey Press Elves

The engaging figures that populate the Abbey Press "elf-help" line of publications and products first appeared in 1987 on the pages of a small self-help book called *Be-good-to-yourself Therapy.* Shaped by the publishing staff's vision and defined in R.W. Alley's inventive illustrations, they lived out author Cherry Hartman's gentle, self-nurturing advice with charm, poignancy, and humor.

Reader response was so enthusiastic that more Elf-help Books were soon under way, a still-growing series that has inspired a line of related gift products.

The especially endearing character featured in the early books—sporting a cap with a mood-changing candle in its peak—has since been joined by a spirited female elf with flowers in her hair.

These two exuberant, sensitive, resourceful, kindhearted, lovable sprites, along with their lively elfin community, reveal what's truly important as they offer messages of joy and wonder, playfulness and co-creation, wholeness and serenity, the miracle of life and the mystery of God's love.

With wisdom and whimsy, these little creatures with long noses demonstrate the elf-help way to a rich and fulfilling life.

Elf-help Books...adding "a little character" and a lot of help to self-help reading!

Anger Therapy (new, improved binding)
#20127-7 $4.95 ISBN 0-87029-292-7

Caregiver Therapy (new, improved binding)
#20164-0 $4.95 ISBN 0-87029-285-4

Self-esteem Therapy (new, improved binding)
#20165-7 $4.95 ISBN 0-87029-280-3

Take-charge-of-your-life Therapy
(new, improved binding)
#20168-1 $4.95 ISBN 0-87029-271-4

Work Therapy (new, improved binding)
#20166-5 $4.95 ISBN 0-87029-276-5

Everyday-courage Therapy
#20167-3 $3.95 ISBN 0-87029-274-9

Peace Therapy
#20176-4 $3.95 ISBN 0-87029-273-0

Friendship Therapy
#20174-9 $3.95 ISBN 0-87029-270-6

Christmas Therapy (color edition)
#20175-6 $5.95 ISBN 0-87029-268-4

Grief Therapy
#20178-0 $3.95 ISBN 0-87029-267-6

More Be-good-to-yourself Therapy
#20180-6 $3.95 ISBN 0-87029-262-5

Happy Birthday Therapy
#20181-4 $3.95 ISBN 0-87029-260-9

Forgiveness Therapy (new, improved binding)
#20184-8 $4.95 ISBN 0-87029-258-7

Keep-life-simple Therapy
#20185-5 $3.95 ISBN 0-87029-257-9

Be-good-to-your-body Therapy
#20188-9 $3.95 ISBN 0-87029-255-2

Celebrate-your-womanhood Therapy
(new, improved binding)
#20189-7 $4.95 ISBN 0-87029-254-4

Acceptance Therapy (color edition)
#20182-2 $5.95 ISBN 0-87029-259-5

Acceptance Therapy (regular edition)
#20190-5 $3.95 ISBN 0-87029-245-5

Keeping-up-your-spirits Therapy
#20195-4 $3.95 ISBN 0-87029-242-0

Play Therapy (new, improved binding)
#20200-2 $4.95 ISBN 0-87029-233-1

Slow-down Therapy
#20203-6 $3.95 ISBN 0-87029-229-3

One-day-at-a-time Therapy
#20204-4 $3.95 ISBN 0-87029-228-5

Prayer Therapy (new, improved binding)
#20206-9 $4.95 ISBN 0-87029-225-0

Be-good-to-your-marriage Therapy
(new, improved binding)
#20205-1 $4.95 ISBN 0-87029-224-2

Be-good-to-yourself Therapy (hardcover)
#20196-2 $10.95 ISBN 0-87029-243-9

Be-good-to-yourself Therapy
(new, improved binding)
#20255-6 $4.95 ISBN 0-87029-209-9

Available at your favorite bookstore or directly from us at One Caring Place, Abbey Press Publications, St. Meinrad, IN 47577.
Phone orders: Call 1-800-325-2511